P9-DVO-816

Hello, Beautiful!

Six-Legged Animals

WORLD
BOOK

www.worldbook.com

World Book, Inc.
180 North LaSalle Street, Suite 900
Chicago, Illinois 60601
USA

For information about other World Book publications, visit our website at www.worldbook.com or call 1-800-WORLDBK (967-5325).

For information about sales to schools and libraries, call 1-800-975-3250 (United States), or 1-800-837-5365 (Canada).

Library of Congress Cataloging-in-Publication Data for this volume has been applied for.

Hello, Beautiful!
ISBN: 978-0-7166-3567-3 (set, hc.)

Six-Legged Animals
ISBN: 978-0-7166-3575-8 (hc.)

Also available as:
ISBN: 978-0-7166-3585-7 (e-book)

Printed in China by Shenzhen Wing King Tong Paper Products Co., Ltd., Shenzhen, Guangdong
1st printing July 2018

Staff

Writer: Grace Guibert

Executive Committee

President
Jim O'Rourke

Vice President and Editor in Chief
Paul A. Kobasa

Vice President, Finance
Donald D. Keller

Vice President, Marketing
Jean Lin

Vice President, International Sales
Maksim Rutenberg

Vice President, Technology
Jason Dole

Director, Human Resources
Bev Ecker

Editorial

Director, New Print
Tom Evans

Managing Editor, New Print
Jeff De La Rosa

Senior Editor, New Print
Shawn Brennan

Editor, New Print
Grace Guibert

Librarian
S. Thomas Richardson

Manager, Contracts & Compliance (Rights & Permissions)
Loranne K. Shields

Manager, Indexing Services
David Pofelski

Digital

Director, Digital Content Development
Emily Kline

Director, Digital Product Development
Erika Meller

Manager, Digital Products
Jonathan Wills

Graphics and Design

Senior Art Director
Tom Evans

Senior Visual Communications Designer
Melanie Bender

Media Researcher
Rosalia Bledsoe

Manufacturing/ Production

Manufacturing Manager
Anne Fritzinger

Proofreader
Nathalie Strassheim

Contents

Introduction

Welcome to "Hello, Beautiful!" picture books!

This book is about six-legged animals called insects. Each book in the "Hello, Beautiful!" series uses large, colorful photographs and a few words to describe our world to children who are not yet reading on their own or are beginning to learn to read. For the benefit of both grown-up and child readers, a picture key is included in the back of the volume to describe each photograph and specific type of animal in more detail.

"Hello, Beautiful!" books can help pre-readers and starting readers get into the habit of having fun with books and learning from them, too. With pre-readers, a grown-up reader (parent, grandparent, librarian, teacher, older brother or sister) can point to the words on each page as he or she speaks them aloud to help the listening child associate the concept of text with the object or idea it describes.

Large, colorful photographs give pre-readers plenty to see while they listen to the reader. If no reader is available, pre-readers can "read" on their own, turning the pages of the book and speaking their own stories about what they see. For new readers, the photographs provide visual hints about the words on the page. Often, these words describe the specific type of animal shown. This animal may not be representative of all species, or types, of that animal.

This book displays some of the insects that live all over the world. Many people think insects are pests, but they are an integral part of functioning ecosystems. Help inspire respect and care for these important and beautiful animals by sharing this "Hello, Beautiful!" book with a child soon.

Ant

Hello, beautiful ant!

You are a red harvester ant. You are small, but you are very strong!

You live with lots of other ants in a big group.

Bee

Hello, beautiful bee!

You are a honey bee. You fly from flower to flower. You sip sweet juice from each flower. You make honey from the juice.

You make yellow wax. You build your home with it!

Beetle

Hello,
beautiful beetle!

You are a giant stag
beetle. You have
a hard shell to
protect your
wings and body.

You have **big** jaws that look like a deer's horns!

Butterfly

Hello, beautiful butterfly!

You are an American lady butterfly. You have big, colorful wings.

You suck juice from flowers with your long, thin mouth!

Caddisfly

Hello, beautiful caddisfly!

You have two pairs of long wings.

You live close to water. You like to fly around at night!

Cicada

Hello, beautiful cicada!

You are a periodical cicada. We hear your buzzing song when you come out in the summer.

You stay in the ground until you are fully grown. That takes 17 years!

Firefly

Hello, beautiful firefly!

You are a big dipper firefly. When it is dark out, you flash your body like a light! This is how you get other fireflies to notice you!

Grasshopper

Hello, beautiful grasshopper!

You are a lubber grasshopper. You have long, strong back legs.

You can **l e a p**
20 times the length
of your body!

Hornet

Hello, beautiful hornet!

You are a European hornet. Your body is **yellow** and **black**.

If we are not careful, you might sting us!

Ladybug

Hello, beautiful ladybug!

You are bright red with black dots.

Your round body is shaped like half of a pea!

25

Mantis

Hello, beautiful mantis!

You are an orchid mantis. Your body is the color and shape of the plants you live on.

You look just like a flower!

Moth

Hello, beautiful moth!

You are an emperor moth. You look a lot like a butterfly!

The spots on your wings scare away other animals!

Picture Key

Learn more about these six-legged animals! Use the picture keys below to learn where each insect lives, how big it grows, and its favorite foods!

Ant

Hello, beautiful ant!

You are a red harvester ant. You are small, but you are very strong!

You live with lots of other ants in a big group.

Bee

Hello, beautiful bee!

You are a honey bee. You fly from flower to flower. You sip sweet juice from each flower. You make honey from the juice.

You make yellow wax. You build your home with it!

Bzzzzzzzz!

Beetle

Hello, beautiful beetle!

You are a giant stag beetle. You have a hard shell to protect your wings and body.

You have big jaws that look like a deer's horns!

Pages 6-7 Ant

The red harvester ant lives mainly in the southwestern United States. Workers range in size from $1/5$ to $1/4$ inch (5 to 7 millimeters) long. The queen reaches $3/5$ to $2/3$ inch (15 to 17 millimeters) in length. Red harvester ants eat mainly seeds.

Pages 8-9 Bee

Honey bees are found on every continent except Antarctica. The worker honey bee is about $1/2$ inch (1.3 centimeters) in length. The queen honey bee can reach up to $4/5$ inch (2 centimeters) in length. Honey bees drink *nectar,* a sweet liquid from flowers.

Pages 10-11 Beetle

The giant stag beetle lives in the southern United States. It has *mandibles* (jaws) 1 inch (2.5 centimeters) long and a body 1 $1/2$ to 2 inches (3.8 to 5 centimeters) long. Giant stag beetles eat plant juices, decaying fruit, and a sweet liquid called *honeydew* produced by insects called *aphids*.

Butterfly

Hello, beautiful butterfly!

You are an American lady butterfly. You have big, colorful wings.

You suck juice from flowers with your long, thin mouth!

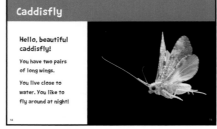

Caddisfly

Hello, beautiful caddisfly!

You have two pairs of long wings.

You live close to water. You like to fly around at night!

Cicada

Hello, beautiful cicada!

You are a periodical cicada. We hear your buzzing song when you come out in the summer.

You stay in the ground until you are fully grown. That takes 17 years!

Pages 12-13 Butterfly

The American lady butterfly lives in the southern United States, Mexico, and Central America south to Colombia. It migrates to temporary homes in the northern United States, southern Canada, the West Indies, and Europe. The wings are about 2 to 3 inches (5 to 7.5 centimeters) across when open. Adult American lady butterflies drink the nectar of flowers. The caterpillar of the American lady feeds on plants such as everlasting flower and cottonweed.

Pages 14-15 Caddisfly

Caddisflies can be found on every continent except Antarctica. They live in and around water. Adults grow to be about 1 $1/4$ inches (3 centimeters) long. Caddisflies sip water, plant juices, or insect honeydew.

Pages 16-17 Cicada

The 17-year periodical cicada (*suh KAY duh* or *suh KAH duh*) is commonly found in the northeastern and midwestern United States. Adults are usually 1 to 2 inches (2.5 to 5 centimeters) long. *Nymphs* (young) feed on roots. Adults feed on tree sap.

Firefly

Hello, beautiful firefly!

You are a big dipper firefly. When it is dark out, you flash your body like a light! This is how you get other fireflies to notice you!

Pages 18-19 Firefly
The big dipper firefly is the most common firefly in North America. It is a type of soft-bodied beetle. Big dipper fireflies are mainly found east of the Rocky Mountains in the United States. These fireflies range in size from $3/8$ to $3/5$ of an inch (9 to 15 millimeters) long. The *larvae* (young) feed on other insect larvae, slugs, and other tiny creatures. Adult big dipper fireflies are not known to eat at all.

Grasshopper

Hello, beautiful grasshopper!

You are a lubber grasshopper. You have long, strong back legs.

You can l e a p 20 times the length of your body!

Pages 20-21 Grasshopper
The lubber grasshopper lives in meadows and fields across the southern United States. Lubbers are among the largest grasshoppers. Adults grow to about 3 inches (8 centimeters). They primarily eat plants.

Hornet

Hello, beautiful hornet!

You are a European hornet. Your body is yellow and black.

If we are not careful, you might sting us!

Pages 22-23 Hornet
The European hornet is originally from Europe and Asia. It was introduced to North America in the 1800's. It builds its nests in hollows in trees or structures. Adult European worker hornets are about 1 $1/4$ inches (3 centimeters) in length. The queen may reach up to 1 $1/3$ inches (3.5 centimeters) in length. European hornets prey on flies, bees, and other insects. They also eat tree sap, fruit, and honeydew.

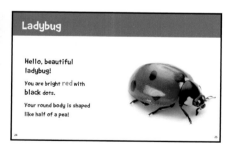

Ladybug

Hello, beautiful ladybug!

You are bright red with black dots.

Your round body is shaped like half of a pea!

Pages 24-25 Ladybug
Ladybugs are a type of beetle. They live in most areas of the world. Ladybugs are up to around $2/5$ inch (1 centimeter) in length. They primarily eat aphids, scale insects, mealybugs, and mites.

Mantis

Hello, beautiful mantis!

You are an orchid mantis. Your body is the color and shape of the plants you live on.

You look just like a flower!

Pages 26-27 Mantis
The orchid mantis lives in the rain forests of Southeast Asia. Male orchid mantises grow to 2.5 inches (6.5 centimeters) long. Female orchid mantises grow up to 7 inches (18 centimeters) long. The orchid mantis eats such small insects as bees, butterflies, and flies.

Moth

Hello, beautiful moth!

You are an emperor moth. You look a lot like a butterfly!

The spots on your wings scare away other animals!

Pages 28-29 Moth
The emperor moth lives in Europe, in open, poorly drained areas known as moors. The male is slightly smaller than the female, with a wingspread of 2 $2/3$ inches (6.8 centimeters) compared to the females' 3 inches (7.8 centimeters). The caterpillars feed on plant leaves. Adult moths do not feed.

Index